GW00778352

Baking with Sourdough

Sara Pitzer

Most of us have known baking only with the recent invention of commercial yeast, but baking with sourdough is being rediscovered. In the days of covered wagons, a pot of sourdough starter for leavening breads, biscuits, and flapjacks was such a common part of cooking that no one would have thought of writing a book of sourdough recipes. During the California Gold Rush and later the Yukon Gold Rush, sourdough was so much a part of their diet that the prospectors were known as "sourdoughs." And before pioneers, prospectors, or even colonists, Columbus brought sourdough to American shores aboard his ship.

Perhaps because of all this, some people have considered sourdough uniquely American. But the Egyptians had it several thousand years before the birth of Christ; the ancient Greeks and Romans used it too.

If you have ever kept leftover mashed potatoes or canned fruit so long it began to ferment, you have an idea of how sourdough must have begun and of why it would have attracted attention. The wild yeasts in the air settle into such congenial environments as sugar, starch and liquid combinations and begin to grow, fermenting and producing potent alcohol which rises to the top. For a long time people were more interested in brewing than baking. Even the American prospectors had uses for the alcohol which surfaced in their sourdough starter pots. They called it "hooch" after the Alaskan Hoochinoo Indians who produced liquor by a sourdough process.

Jokes about hooch permeate American humor, along with stories about the prospector who used sourdough starter to glue broken furniture, the hunter who used it to polish the brass on his gun, and the pioneer mother who rubbed her children with a combination of sourdough and shoe polish so they would rise and shine.

Considering how much people talked about sourdough, it is not surprising that a number of misconceptions about it developed and survive even today.

Perhaps the most common misconception is that sourdough starter should not be frozen. Because the prospectors believed this, they faithfully took their starter pots into their bedrolls with them at night so body heat would keep the starter from freezing. Even Irma Rombauer and Marion R. Becker, authors of the modern classic, *Joy of Cooking*, warn readers that freezing will kill sourdough starter. The fact is, heat over 95°F will kill the yeast, but it can be kept frozen almost indefinitely and is perfectly usable as soon as it has been thawed. Freezing is probably the best way to maintain a seldom-used starter.

Another unfortunate misconception about sourdough is that it is finicky and that baking with it requires an almost scientifically controlled environment. Obviously that can't be true or it would not have flourished on wagon trains and at prospecting sites where no one had much control over temperature or time. It's hard to imagine an old "sourdough" cutting short a successful panning session because it was time to bake the bread.

Another widely held, but mistaken, idea is that anything baked with sourdough tastes so sour it puckers your mouth. Actually, sourdough products can be as bland or as sour as you wish.

On the other hand, one thing you may have heard about sourdough is true: Using it takes time. Fortunately it's not your time; because sourdough needs more time to work as a leavener, you must begin the baking process further ahead of when you want to finish than you would with commercial yeast or baking powder. That's the main way sourdough baking differs from other kinds. You have to give sourdough time to grow, you have to keep it alive, and — of course — you have to catch the wild yeast to have a starter.

Catching a Starter

You can get a starter in any one of four ways. The easiest is to take advantage of someone else's catch and scrounge a tablespoon or so of starter from a flourishing pot. Old-timers preferred this way because their only alternative was the most difficult method — traping some wild yeast from the air and growing it into a starter, which could taste wonderful or terrible, depending on the quality of the catch. In winter, catching any yeast at all was unlikely because everything was frozen into inactivity and catching a good wild yeast for a starter is as difficult now as ever. Some bakers believe you'll do better if you try in warm weather in a kitchen where many loaves of bread have been baked, because leftover yeast spores might be floating in the air.

Two simpler ways of creating a starter are now possible. One is to use commercial yeast, growing it in flour and water and essentially letting it become wild again; the other is to buy a culture from long established vendor. Specialty and natural food stores often sell them, or you could try looking online. Sourdoughs International (208-382-4828; www.sourdo.com) in Cascade, Idaho, carries starters from around the world. King Arthur Flour (800-827-6836; www. kingarthurflour.com) carries French and New England sourdough starters, and for taste of authentic Oregon Trail sourdough, contact the friends of the late Carl Griffith, an enthusiast who shared his family's starter throughout his lifetime (http://carlsfriends.net; CarlsFriends@att.net).

Once you have your starter, whether it was purchased, received from a friend, or grown wild, you are ready to try these recipes.

STARTING FROM SCRATCH

4   **cups unbleached white flour**
2   **teaspoons salt**
2   **tablespoons honey**
4   **cups potato water**

Mix all the ingredients together in a large, non-metal container. The container should be large enough to allow the mixture to more than double in bulk. Let the mixture stand, loosely covered, in a warm place (about 85°F is ideal). In two or three days either the mixture will begin to froth, expand, and smell sour, or it will mold and smell worse. If the first happens, you have captured wild yeast and created your own starter. Let it season a couple of days in the refrigerator and then try baking with it to see if you like its flavor. (You may not. Some yeasts will leaven but they taste terrible.)

If you end up with a smelly, moldy bowl of flour and water, not a sign of bubble or froth to be seen, the catch has eluded you. Throw the mess away and try again, or try one of the other methods for getting a starter. The following recipe is more certain because it begins with dried or "domesticated" yeast. The starter you produce will still be a sourdough, even though its origins are domestic. After a while, the difference in taste will be minor.

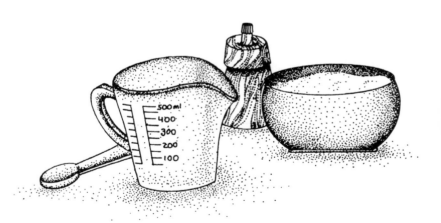

DRIED YEAST STARTER

1   package active dried yeast
2   cups unbleached white flour
1½ cups warm water
1   tablespoon honey

Mix the ingredients thoroughly in a non-metal container large enough to allow the mixture to double, or even (because of the dried yeast) triple. Let the mixture stand, loosely covered, for a day or two, until it is frothy and full of bubbles. The bubbling will begin shortly after you mix the ingredients, but it will take a longer time for the bubbles to permeate the mixture and for the sour smell characteristic of sourdough to develop.

After the mixture has fermented and soured, stir it down and refrigerate. It will be better after it has aged a few days in the refrigerator, and after having been used and replenished for a week or so will be better yet.

WHOLE WHEAT STARTER

1   package active dried yeast
1   cup whole wheat flour
1   cup warm water
1   tablespoon sugar

Mix the ingredients together in a non-metal container large enough to allow the mixture to expand to as much as three times its original bulk. Cover the container loosely and let it stand, to bubble and ferment, in a warm place. Once the mixture has developed a slightly sour smell (about a day), refrigerate until you are ready to use it.

When you begin a starter in smaller amounts, as with this whole wheat starter, or when you find you are using your starter so often it hardly has time to ferment, you may need to expand your existing starter.

Expanding the Starter

To expand the amount of starter, simply add equal amounts of flour and water to it, let it stand to ferment until it is bubbling and sour, then refrigerate. For the truest sourdough taste, allow the expanded starter to age in the refrigerator a day or two before you use it, but if you are interested more in the leavening than in the flavoring qualities of the starter, you can use it at once. Some bakers keep two or more pots going so they can choose between a mild starter and an older, more pungent one, depending on what they are going to bake and how they want it to taste.

The rising power of the starter is the result of the yeast's breaking down the starches to produce alcohol (hooch) and carbon dioxide bubbles. Those bubbles are the leaven. If your starter, expanded or not, has sat too long without new food for its yeast being added, it will become overly sour and will lose its ability to leaven.

Sweetening the Pot

To revive an over-aged starter, you need to sweeten the pot. When old-time western gamblers picked up that term, meaning to add more money to the pot, they must have been influenced by the sweetening process used to revive sickly starter. Simply throw away all but a few spoonsful of the old starter, wash the pot, and then mix the old starter with 2 cups each of flour and warm water. Let the mixture stand at room temperature until it bubbles and foams, as you did when beginning the original starter. When you can see that the mixture is active, growing, and full of bubbles, return it to the refrigerator. For truest sourdough flavor let it age a day or so before you use it again. And next time, remember to feed the starter a little sooner or, if you're not going to use the starter for a while, freeze it.

Using your starter regularly keeps it in good shape because when you use it you should also replenish (a kind of feeding) the pot.

Replenishing the Pot

Replenishing is merely a matter of putting into the pot about the same amounts of flour and water as you take out. If, for instance, you use one-half to one cup of starter, stir in about a cup of flour and a little less than a cup of water. The exact amounts don't matter; the idea is to maintain approximately the same amount of starter all the time, by replacing what you've used with fresh flour and water. Keeping a starter in good condition and following a few common sense rules guarantee successful sourdough baking.

Rules for Success

- Avoid metal utensils when working with sourdough because sourdough can be corrosive. (Remember those prospectors polished their brass with it.)
- Make sure all utensils are clean so you don't encourage the growth of some bacteria left over from last night's supper.
- Use all ingredients at room temperature.
- Choose storage containers and mixing bowls large enough to allow for expansion to more than double in bulk, and never cover any sourdough container tightly. Not only does the starter need air to live, but also expanding starter could burst the container.
- Incubate your starter and set bread to rise in a draft-free place where the temperature is at least 80°F. and no more than 95°F. That is no problem in an Alabama summer, but in a cool climate, finding a continuously warm spot takes some doing. One of the simplest solutions is to make an incubator by placing a heating pad turned on low inside a styrofoam picnic chest. Use a rack or wooden trivet to hold the pot of starter above the heating pad, and keep a thermometer on top of the loosely covered bowl to monitor the temperature. You can adjust the temperature slightly by how tightly you settle the lid onto the styrofoam chest.

Keep these few rules about sourdough in mind as you follow the basic procedures which are typical of working with sourdough and differ slightly from other kinds of baking.

Basic Procedures

Time is a key element in sourdough baking. Each step in the preparation process, except for the actual baking, takes longer than it would if you were using commercial yeast or baking powder. Often you need to start as much as a day ahead of the time you want to bake, and always at least several hours ahead. Unless otherwise specified in a recipe, the starter is mixed with some other ingredients and that mixture allowed to ferment. (If you are baking a kneaded bread this is called making a sponge. Interestingly, the sponge step continued in baking after commercial yeast became common, which made the step unnecessary. Only recently have cookbooks begun instructing the baker to go directly from mixing to kneading.)

The length of time the sponge stands will determine the bread's sourness. The longer the sponge mixture stands before the rest of the ingredients are worked in, the more sour your bread will be. The sponge mixture will leaven as soon as it is growing, foamy and full of bubbles. If you use it just a few hours after setting it out, you can bake goods with only the mildest sourdough flavor. If you allow the mixture to stand for a full 24 hours or more, the resulting products will be increasingly sour.

A sponge which stands *too* long can begin to lose its leavening power as the yeast uses up the available nutrients and has no more starch or sugar to break down into alcohol and carbon dioxide. It's better to use a sponge within four hours of the time it's become fully permeated with tiny bubbles, but even that timing is not as critical as it sounds, because when you do add more ingredients, the yeast will have more food and will start to grow again, leavening the bread as it does.

Using time to control flavor does not produce results as predictable as those from baking powder or commercial yeast. With sourdough, the taste may be a bit different, even with the same recipe, each time you bake.

While you cannot control flavor exactly, you can control texture surprisingly well. Again time is your tool. Generally, people find sourdough breads moister and coarser than other breads. If you want a fine-grained texture, allow the dough to rise twice in the bowl, punching it down between risings. This adds about an hour to the overall rising time in the bowl. If you prefer a coarse texture, allow the loaf to rise *almost* to the point of falling in the pans before baking. This adds about half an hour.

The moisture of the bread can also be controlled by time. If your first loaves seem too dry, shorten the baking time; if too moist, lengthen it.

All sourdoughs rise more slowly than breads made with commercial yeast, but can be speeded up a little with extra warmth, though never over 95°F. Because of the slower rising, it's a good idea to cover the bowl or pans with a damp cloth so a crust will not form on top of the dough and retard rising. Also, you can't count on as much rising in the oven, once baking has begun, as you can with commercial yeast and baking powder, so allow your dough to come to nearly its finished size before putting the pans into the oven where the heat will kill the yeast and stop the rising.

Adapting Standard Recipes

As you become accustomed to the subtleties in sourdough taste and texture, you may want to go beyond the scope of recipes here — beyond any sourdough recipes you can find anywhere — to experiment with converting some of your other recipes to sourdough. Using sourdough starter to replace regular yeast or baking powder in recipes is simpler than it sounds and does not require elaborate conversion charts.

To adapt a yeast recipe, begin with a small amount of starter, about ¼ cup for recipes using less than 6 cups of flour and about ½ cup for recipes calling for more flour. Mix the starter with some of the flour and some of the liquid from the basic recipe you want to convert. Figure that ¼ cup starter has replaced about ¼ cup flour and slightly less than ¼ cup liquid in the recipe. If you use ½ cup starter, figure it has replaced ½ cup flour and a little less than ½ cup liquid, and so on. In baking powder recipes figure the same way, but use as much as a cup of starter even in recipes calling for only 2 or 3 cups of flour.

Allow the mixture of starter, flour and liquid — the sponge — to stand and bubble for 4 to 24 hours, depending on the sourness you want. With quick breads you can shorten the time so the mixture stands only until it is obviously active, as little as an hour, if you're not trying for the sour taste. When ready to bake, proceed with the recipe, adjusting the amounts of flour and liquid according to the amount of starter you used. Add as much flour as necessary to get a dough you can knead or a batter (for quick breads) that seems about as thick as the recipe was before you adapted it to sourdough.

Go through the usual kneading, rising, and shaping steps for yeast breads. For quick breads, pour the batter into the pan and allow to stand until it begins to rise. Then bake as usual.

The only tricky part in making these adaptations is deciding which flavors are enhanced in combination with sourdough and which are not. Try to *imagine* how the flavors you're contemplating would taste together. If it "thinks good," try it.

Using the sourdough recipes in this bulletin will give you a feel for how sourdough starter works in kneaded and quick breads. Once you get used to it, you'll find it surprisingly easy to use sourdough in your own favorite recipes.

About the Recipes

These recipes generally call for unbleached white flour or for one of the whole grain flours. When you can get it, hard wheat flour, sometimes sold as "bread flour," works well for kneaded breads; all purpose flour works best for quick breads and pancakes. If you can not find specially milled hard wheat flour or don't want to pay the extra cost of buying flours from natural foods stores, you can still bake wonderful sourdough products. All these recipes have been tested with ordinary, unbleached white, all purpose flour — the kind sold in grocery stores everywhere — and you can produce excellent baked goods using it.

Also, most of the recipes here include neither commercial yeast nor baking powder because they are unnecessary. If your starter is in good condition, your baked goods will rise without extra help. However, a few of the recipes use sourdough more for its flavor than for its leavening power. Whether you try them or not will depend on why you are interested in sourdough. Some people want to avoid what they fear to be the harmful effects of baking powder. Some Benedictine sisters want to produce a leavened altar bread made only of flour and water. Probably most of us simply want the fun, challenge and good taste of stalking the wild yeast.

SOURDOUGH WHITE SANDWICH BREAD

This fine-grained bread has a tender crust and delicate texture because it's made with milk and allowed to rise twice before being shaped into loaves.

1	cup sourdough starter
1¼	cups unbleached white flour
1	cup warm water
1½	cups milk
2	tablespoons honey
2	teaspoons salt
2	tablespoons butter
6	½ cups unbleached white flour, approximately

Mix the first 3 ingredients in a large bowl and allow to stand in a warm place so the mixture can ferment and bubble for 10 to 24 hours. When you are ready to bake the bread, heat the milk, add honey, salt and butter to it and cool the mixture to lukewarm.

When the liquid mixture reaches room temperature, mix in the sourdough mixture; then beat in enough flour to make a dough you can handle. Turn the dough out onto a floured board, cover with a damp cloth and allow to rest for 15 to 20 minutes before kneading. Knead until the dough is smooth and elastic. Don't skimp on kneading time with this recipe.

After kneading, place the dough in a greased bowl and allow to rise until doubled in bulk. Cover the bowl with a damp cloth which will keep a crust from forming on the dough. Once the dough has doubled, punch it down, cover again with a damp cloth and allow to rise a second time to double. Each of these risings may take as long as 2 hours. When the dough has doubled a second time, knead it down and shape into 2 or 3 loaves, depending on the size of your pans. The dough should fill each greased pan by about half. Brush the loaves with melted butter, cover them with a damp cloth, and place in a warm spot to rise until double in bulk. This usually takes about an hour, but could take longer, depending on temperature.

Bake in a preheated 375°F oven for about 45 minutes, or until the loaves are nicely browned, pull away from the sides of the pans, and sound hollow when tapped.

For the most tender crust, brush the loaves with butter again and cover lightly with a dry cloth as they cool.

SOURDOUGH WHITE BREAD PLUS

This bread is nice and chewy and stays fresh for a long time. It's especially good for sandwiches because of its fine grain. Soy grits and wheat germ enhance its nutritional value.

1	cup sourdough starter
1¼	cups unbleached white flour
1	cup warm water
2	tablespoons melted butter
¼	cup honey
2	teaspoons salt
⅓	cup soy grits
⅓	cup raw wheat germ
2½	cups unbleached white flour, approximately

Mix the first three ingredients in a large bowl, cover loosely and allow to ferment for 10 to 24 hours. When ready to bake, add the cooled melted butter, honey and salt. Beat well. Add the wheat germ and soy grits and beat again. Then beat in more flour as needed to make a dough you can handle. Turn the dough out onto a floured board, cover it with a damp cloth and let it stand for about 15 minutes, then knead until smooth and elastic.

Place the kneaded dough in a large greased bowl, cover with a damp cloth and place in a warm spot to rise until dough is doubled in bulk. This will probably take at least 2 hours, depending on the temperature. Once the dough has doubled, you can either punch it down and allow to rise again, for finest texture, or you can shape the loaves after the first rising. Either way, place the loaves in greased loaf pans (the 8x5 inch size will make 2 loaves), cover with a damp cloth and allow to rise until the dough is nearly the size the finished loaf should be — about double the starting bulk. Bake in a preheated 350°F oven for an hour, or until the loaves are brown, have pulled away from the sides of the pans, and sound hollow when tapped.

You can use any size pan you wish as long as the dough fills the pan only halfway. For smaller pans you may have to decrease the baking time slightly.

SOURDOUGH FRENCH-STYLE WHITE BREAD

1   cup sourdough starter
2   cups warm water
4   cups unbleached white flour
2   teaspoons salt
2   teaspoons sugar
4   cups unbleached white flour, approximately

Mix the first 3 ingredients until smooth in a large bowl. Cover loosely and allow to stand in a warm place to ferment and bubble of 10 to 24 hours, depending on how sour you want the bread to be.

When ready to bake the bread, stir in the salt and sugar and enough flour to make a dough you can handle. Form the dough into a ball, cover with a damp cloth and allow to stand 15 to 20 minutes, then knead until smooth and elastic, adding more flour as necessary. The dough should be quite stiff so it will hold its shape.

Put the kneaded dough in a greased bowl, cover with a damp cloth and allow to rise until doubled in bulk, then shape into 2 long loaves and place on a cookie sheet which you have sprinkled with corn meal. Allow to rise until the loaves have doubled in bulk. You may want to brush them from time to time with cool water to prevent a crust forming on top. It's not a good idea to use a damp cloth on top of these loaves. The loaves tend to flatten out from the weight since there are no pan sides to support the cloth and hold the loaves in.

Just before baking, brush the loaves with cold water and bake in a preheated 450°F oven for 30 to 35 minutes, or until the loaves are lightly browned and sound hollow when tapped.

For the look of traditional sourdough French bread, brush the loaves several times during baking with a cooled mixture of 1 teaspoon cornstarch boiled in ½ cup water, and slash the tops of the loaves diagonally several times with a razor after the first 10 minutes of baking. For the most crusty bread possible, slide a pan of hot water into the oven along with the loaves. And, when cooling, you will get a crisper crust if you leave the loaves uncovered.

FRENCH-STYLE SOURDOUGH BREAD
WITH WHOLE WHEAT

Even people who ordinarily don't like whole wheat like this bread. It's especially good with stews, cheese fondue and baked beans.

½	cup starter
5	cups unbleached white flour
2	tablespoons oil
1	tablespoon honey
4½	cups warm water
5	cups whole wheat flour
1	tablespoon salt
3 to 5	cups unbleached white flour

Combine the first 5 ingredients in a large bowl. Cover loosely and allow to stand in a warm place 5 to 10 hours. The longer this sponge stands, the more sour the bread will be. When ready to make the bread, add the whole wheat flour and salt and mix well. Then gradually work in as much unbleached white flour as you need to make a dough you can handle.

Form the dough into a ball, cover with a damp cloth and allow to stand 15 to 20 minutes before kneading. Knead until smooth and elastic, place in a large, greased bowl in a warm place and allow to rise until double in bulk. If it is not convenient to take the bread when it has doubled, punch down the dough and allow to rise again. When ready to bake, shape the dough into 5 long, skinny "ropes" and arrange them on a cookie sheet sprinkled heavily with corn meal. Put the loaves in a *warm* oven. When the bread starts to rise, turn the oven to 400°F and bake until the crust is brown — about 25 minutes. For a traditional French look, slash the loaves 3 times each before baking; for heavier crust brush the loaves with cold water once or twice during the baking period and cool them, uncovered, on a rack.

SOURDOUGH PUMPERNICKEL

¾ cup sourdough starter
1 cup unbleached white flour
¾ cup water
1½ cups milk
2 cups whole wheat flour
2 teaspoons salt
¾ cup corn meal
2½ cups rye flour, approximately

Mix together the first 3 ingredients in a large bowl, cover loosely and allow to ferment in a warm place for at least 10 hours, longer if you want a sour pumpernickel. When you are ready to bake, mix the milk (which should be lukewarm) into the fermented starter mixture, then beat in the whole wheat flour, salt and corn meal. Next, work in as much rye flour as needed to make a dough you can handle. Shape it into a ball, cover with a damp cloth and allow to stand for about 20 minutes before you try to knead it. This bread is difficult to knead and you may find it easier if you grease your hands well before beginning.

When the dough is thoroughly kneaded, place it in a greased bowl, turning it once so the top of the ball of dough is also greased. Set the dough in a warm place, covered with a damp cloth, to rise. This bread will rise slowly because it is heavy, so allow at least an hour, possibly longer. When the dough feels light and puffy, even if it has not quite doubled in bulk, knead it down and form into a round loaF Put the loaf on a cookie sheet which has been heavily sprinkled with corn meal, grease the top of the loaf with soft butter, and place in a warm spot to rise until nearly double. This will probably take at least an hour.

Bake in a preheated 375°F oven for about 40 minutes, or until the loaf sounds hollow when you tap it.

This makes a very dense loaf; if you would prefer it a little more springy, substitute unbleached white flour for some of the whole wheat flour and be sure to allow plenty of rising time before baking.

MOLASSES RYE BREAD

If you like a slightly sweet, chewy bread, this may turn out to be your favorite recipe. The combination of sourdough tang and molasses produces a sweet-sour taste you can't accomplish any other way.

1	cup sourdough starter
2	cups unbleached white flour
1	cup water
2	cups rye flour
2	cups boiling water
¾	cup dark molasses
⅓	cup butter
2	teaspoons salt
5	cups unbleached white flour, approximately

Mix the first 3 ingredients in a large bowl, cover loosely and allow to stand in a warm place. The mixture will ferment and bubble.

When you are ready to bake the bread, combine the rye flour, boiling water, molasses, butter and salt in a large bowl. When the mixture has cooled to barely warm, stir in sourdough mixture with a wooden spoon. Then stir in as much unbleached white flour as you need to make a dough you can handle. Turn it out onto a floured board and work into a ball. Cover the ball with a damp cloth and let it rest for 15 to 30 minutes, then knead until smooth and elastic. Place the kneaded dough in a large greased bowl and allow to rise until doubled in bulk — about 2 to 3 hours. Punch down and either allow to rise again, for finest texture, or form at once into 3 round loaves.

Put the loaves on a cookie sheet which you have sprinkled heavily with corn meal. Allow the loaves to rise until doubled in bulk. Bake in a preheated 350°F oven for 50 to 60 minutes. For a more chewy crust, brush the loaves with cold water before putting them in the oven.

SOURDOUGH BANANA BREAD

1½ cups sourdough starter
1   cup sugar
1   teaspoon baking soda
1   teaspoon salt
⅓   cup butter
1   beaten egg
1   cup unbleached white flour
1   cup very ripe mashed banana
½   cup chopped nuts

Bring the starter to room temperature in a large bowl. When it has begun to bubble, add the sugar, soda and salt to it. Melt and cool the butter and add it, along with the egg, flour and banana, stirring in each ingredient in the order given. When everything is well mixed, stir in the nuts. Pour the batter into a greased loaf pan large enough so that it is no more than two-thirds full. Allow to stand in a warm place for about 20 minutes, then bake in a preheated 350°F oven for at least an hour, or until the loaf tests done when poked with a toothpick. You may lay a piece of brown paper or aluminum foil loosely over the top of the loaf if it is getting too brown. Do not underbake this bread; it will be quite moist even when fully done. Allow it to cool in the pan for about 15 minutes before taking it out. Then allow the loaf to cool completely before trying to slice it. This banana bread will be even better the second day if you have stored it wrapped in foil or plastic wrap.

For the lunch box pack sandwiches made of banana bread spread with a filling of cream cheese and chopped dates.

SOURDOUGH SKILLET BISCUITS

"These must be what made sourdough famous," said a man tasting these biscuits for the first time. They're so crunchy on the outside, light on the inside, that it is hard to believe flour and water are the only main ingredients. If you are using sourdough to avoid baking powder, this recipe is not for you, but if you are looking for an uncommonly good biscuit which is almost embarrassingly easy to make, try this recipe.

2	cups sourdough starter
2	cups all purpose unbleached white flour
1	teaspoon sugar
1	tablespoon baking powder
½	teaspoon salt

Let the starter come to room temperature in a large bowl. It won't hurt the starter to stand for several hours if you should be delayed. About an hour before you want to serve the biscuits, sift the dry ingredients together into the starter bowl and mix to make a firm dough. Pinch off pieces of the dough and gently shape into balls about the size of large walnuts or small eggs. Arrange them in a well-greased 12-inch iron skillet and place in a warm place for 15 to 20 minutes, or long enough for the biscuits to show signs of rising. Because of the baking powder reacting with the sourdough starter this happens fast. Bake in a preheated 400°F oven for about 30 minutes, or until well browned and crusty. Serve hot.

Sourdough Skillet Biscuit Variations

- After sifting in the dry ingredients, add ¼ cup bacon bits which have been fried until crisp and drained. Mix them in as you are mixing in the order dry ingredients.
- Work in ¼ cup chopped onion, which has been sautéed in a small amount of butter, as you mix in the dry ingredients.
- Brush the unbaked biscuits with extra melted butter and shake on paprika and chili powder before baking.
- Mix in 2 tablespoons dried parsley after you add the dry ingredients.
- For breakfast biscuits, spread 2 tablespoons soft butter, 2 tablespoons brown sugar and 1 teaspoon cinnamon in the bottom of the skillet before putting in the biscuit dough. To serve, turn all the biscuits out of the pan and allow the syrup to run over them.

SOURDOUGH BROWN BISCUITS

These biscuits, like the previous ones, contain some baking powder. And like the previous biscuit recipe, this one is easier than most because the shortening does not have to be cut in, thus eliminating a step.

2   cups sourdough starter
1   tablespoon honey
½   teaspoon salt
2   tablespoons oil
2   teaspoons baking powder
1½   cups whole wheat flour

Put the 2 cups starter in a large bowl, cover loosely and allow to stand for at least 10 hours in a warm place. When ready to bake, mix honey, salt and oil into starter. Sift in the baking powder and whole wheat flour. For finest texture, discard any bran which remains in the sifter, but for a heartier biscuit dump the bran right into the mixing bowl with the other ingredients. Mix everything well, but do not over-beat.

Knead the dough gently until it holds together, then roll it out to a thickness of ½ to 1 inch, depending on whether you want thin crusty biscuits or high, lighter ones.

Cut the biscuits out with a cutter or a small can from which both ends have been removed. On a greased cookie sheet place them close together for soft biscuits or leave them farther apart for more crust.

Cover the biscuits with a dry, lightweight cloth and put them in a warm place for about half an hour, or until you see definite signs of rising. Then bake in a preheated 400°F oven for about 20 minutes. Break open one biscuit to be sure they are cooked through.

The nutty taste and crusty texture of these biscuits make them ideal to serve with creamed chipped beef.

OLD-FASHIONED PANCAKES

½   cup sourdough starter
1   cup undiluted evaporated milk
1¾ cups unbleached white flour
1   cup water
2   eggs
2   tablespoons sugar
½   teaspoon salt
1   teaspoon baking soda

Combine the first 4 ingredients in a large bowl, cover loosely and allow stand in a warm place overnight, or for at least 8 hours. Beat together the eggs, sugar, salt and soda, and stir into the starter combination with a wooden spoon. At this point, don't beat. Bake the pancakes on a lightly greased griddle, turning when bubbles appear. These pancakes are quite fat and fluffy and very tender because of the reaction of the soda with the sourdough. If you want them to be thinner, stir in a little more water as you are adding the egg mixture.

To make sourdough waffles stir in 2 or 3 tablespoons of melted butter or cooking oil after all the other ingredients have been added. Bake on a lightly greased waffle iron. The fat added to the batter should help prevent the waffles from sticking provided the iron has been well seasoned.

Variations: Whether you make waffles or pancakes, this recipe lends itself well to the addition of some nutritional reinforcement. A quarter cup toasted wheat germ added with the egg mixture will give a nutty taste and increase the food value of the recipe. For even heartier pancakes, add ¼ to ½ cup chopped pecans before baking.

SOURDOUGH BUCKWHEATS

This is the classic sourdough pancake. Some people keep a separate buckwheat starter just for baking buckwheat pancakes, but it really isn't necessary. Some recipes use buckwheat flavor, thus the white flour in this recipe. If you are fond of a strong buckwheat taste, reduce the amount of white flour you use.

½   cup sourdough starter
1   cup unbleached white flour
1   cup buckwheat flour
2   cups warm water
2   beaten eggs
2   tablespoons sugar
½   teaspoon salt
½   teaspoon baking powder
3   tablespoons melted butter
½   teaspoon baking soda dissolved in 1 tablespoon water

Mix together first 4 ingredients in a large bowl. Beat well. Cover loosely and allow to stand overnight or for at least 8 hours in a warm place. When ready to bake the pancakes, stir in the beaten eggs, sugar, salt, baking powder and melted butter. Finally, stir in the baking soda dissolved in water. Do not stir again after adding the soda. Bake on a moderately hot griddle, taking care not to let the buckwheats burn.

For darker pancakes with a truly old-time taste, allow the batter to age longer than 8 hours and substitute molasses for the 2 table-spoons of sugar.

APPLE MUFFIINS

These muffins are unusually hearty beause they contain some whole wheat flour.

1	cup sourdough starter
1¼	cups unbleached white flour
1	cup water
¾	cup whole wheat flour
⅓	cup powdered milk
½	cup brown sugar
2	teaspoons baking powder
1	teaspoon cinnamon
½	teaspoon salt
¼	cup butter
1	beaten egg
½	cup chopped, peeled apple
¼	cup chopped nuts

Combine the first 3 ingredients in a large bowl, cover loosely and allow to stand in a warm place up to 24 hours, depending on how sour you want the muffins to taste. When ready to bake, sift together all the dry ingredients into a second bowl and cut in the butter until the mixture resembles coarse meal. Add the egg to the starter mixture and stir it quickly into the dry mixture. Do not beat; stir only enough to mix everything. The butter will be lumpy. Fold in the chopped apple and nuts and pour the batter into well greased muffin tins, filling each cup no more than three-quarters full.

Place the tins in a warm place and allow the muffins to rise for about 20 minutes, then bake in a preheated 400°F oven for about 30 minutes. Do not underbake.

SOURDOUGH PRETZELS

These pretzels are absolutely delicious. They're the kind you sometimes can buy from street vendors in cities, and they're wonderful with a little mild yellow mustard squirted on just before you eat them.

¾ cup sourdough starter
¾ cup unbleached white flour
½ cup water
2 tablespoons butter
3 tablespoons sugar
2 teaspoons salt
1 cup hot water
5½ cups unbleached white flour, approximately
1 egg yolk
2 tablespoons heavy cream
Coarse salt

Combine the first 3 ingredients in a large bowl, cover loosely and allow to stand in a warm place at least 8 hours. When ready to make the pretzels, dissolve the butter, sugar and salt in the hot water and cool to lukewarm. When the water is cool enough, add it to the starter mixture and gradually beat in 4 cups of flour. When the dough is stiff and well mixed, turn it out onto a floured board and knead in more flour until you have a very stiff dough. This will be easier to do if you let it rest a few minutes covered with a damp cloth before you begin kneading. Put the dough in a greased bowl, turn once to grease the dough and cover with a damp cloth. Put the bowl in a warm place and allow the dough to rise for 2 hours.

Shape pieces of dough into long ropes, then twist the ropes into pretzel shapes on a greased cookie sheet. Brush the pretzels with a mixture of the beaten egg yolk and cream. Cover with a damp cloth and allow to rise in a warm place for about half an hour. Brush with the egg mixture again, sprinkle with salt and bake about 15 minutes in a preheated 425°F oven.

Cool the pretzels before serving because they'll be gummy when they're hot.

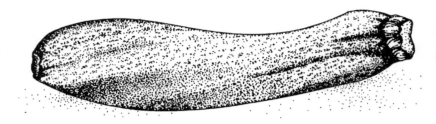

SOURDOUGH ZUCCHINI BREAD

Here's a quick bread recipe for mid-summer when zucchini takes over the land, causing frugal cooks and gardeners to whip up everything from zucchini tarts to zucchini ice cream sundaes to keep from wasting any of the prolific squash. This zucchini bread is similar to the standard quick zucchini breads you may have tasted, except the sourdough gives it a definitive tang and makes it a more moist loaf.

½ cup oil
¾ cup brown sugar
1 egg
½ cup sourdough starter
½ cup milk
1 cup grated zucchini squash
2 cups unbleached white flour
½ teaspoon each baking powder and baking soda
½ teaspoon salt
1 teaspoon cinnamon
¼ teaspoon ground cloves (optional)
¼ cup raisins
¼ cup chopped nuts

Mix the oil, sugar, egg, starter, and milk together in a large bowl. Stir until the sugar is fairly well dissolved. Add the grated zucchini and mix well. Sift the dry ingredients together into the zucchini mixture. Gently fold in the raisins and nuts.

Turn this batter into a greased and floured loaf pan large enough that the mixture does not fill it by more than two-thirds. Bake in a 325°F preheated oven for about an hour, or until the loaf tests done when you poke it with a toothpick. Cool at least 5 minutes before removing the loaf from the pan, then cool completely on a rack. For best flavor and texture, wrap the loaf after it is completely cooled and do not cut it until the next day.

BLUEBERRY BREAKFAST BREAD

1   cup sourdough starter
¼   cup soft shortening
¾   cup sugar
1   egg
½   cup milk
1   cup unbleached white flour
½   teaspoon baking soda
½   teaspoon salt
1   cup blueberries

Bring the starter to room temperature in a large bowl. In another bowl, cream the shortening and sugar together and then beat in the egg and milk. Turn this mixture into the bowl with the sourdough starter and sift in the flour, salt and soda. Mix very well. Gently fold in the blueberries. If they are canned be sure to drain them thoroughly before using. Pour the batter into a well greased 8-inch square pan and allow to stand in a warm place for at least 20 minutes. Meanwhile, prepare the topping:

⅓   cup brown sugar
⅓   cup flour
½   teaspoon cinnamon
¼   cup soft butter

Stir all these ingredients together with a fork until the mixture is crumbly. Sprinkle the topping over the bread batter just before baking in a preheated 375°F oven for 45 to 50 minutes. Do not underbake as this is a moist bread. It will pull away from the sides of the pan when done, although some of the sugar topping may cling to the sides.

This bread smells as though it should be eaten hot, but it is sticky and gummy until it has cooled completely, so keep eager snitchers away until the bread is cold. Then serve cut in squares. It's especially good with a huge glass of cold milk.

MOLASSES-DATE BARS

1	cup sourdough starter
1	beaten egg
½	cup butter
¼	cup brown sugar
¾	cup dark molasses
½	teaspoon salt
1	teaspoon cinnamon
¼	teaspoon baking soda
1⅓	cups unbleached white flour
½	cup chopped dates
2	tablespoons flour

In a large bowl allow the starter to warm up and become active. It should stand at room temperature for 1 to 2 hours. Then add the beaten egg, softened butter, brown sugar and molasses. Beat thoroughly with a wooden spoon. Next, put in the salt, cinnamon and soda. Sift in the flour. Beat the butter until it is lump-free.

Roll the chopped dates in the 2 tablespoons of flour or mix them with the flour in a bowl so they do not stick together. Gently stir them into the beaten batter.

Pour the batter into a well greased 9-inch square pan and bake in a preheated 375°F oven for about 30 minutes or until the batter tests done when poked with a toothpick.

Allow to cool slightly before cutting into bars, then finish cooling on wire racks and sprinkle with powdered sugar before serving. Like most sourdough products, these bars taste much better cold than they do while still warm from the oven.

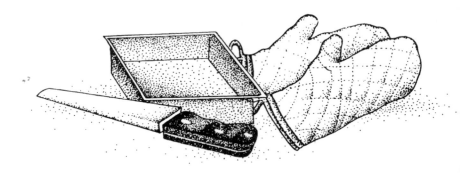

SOURDOUGH POULTRY DRESSING

If you have odds and ends of sourdough breads and biscuits which have gotten stale, save them in your freezer until you have enough to make this poultry stuffing. Once you've tried it, you may decide it's good enough to warrant setting aside some of your bread especially for making dressing. Any sourdough white or whole wheat breads and biscuits are suitable for the dressing, but if you use rye breads, avoid those containing molasses.

6 to 8	cups sourdough bread shreds
	Chicken broth or boullion
¼	cup butter
1	cup celery chopped fine
½	cup chopped onion
¼	cup oil
12 to 16	ounces raw mushrooms, chopped coarsely
1	tablespoon poultry seasoning
1	teaspoon salt
½	teaspoon thyme
½	teaspoon ground black pepper

Put the torn up bread into a large bowl. If it is very stale and dry, pour ½ cup or so chicken broth or boullion over it to soften. The bread should be slightly soft but not sopping wet.

In a large skillet, melt the butter. In it sauté the chopped celery and onion until they are soft but not browned. Pour this on to the bread shreds. Next, heat the oil in the same skillet until it is hot but not smoking. Put in the chopped mushrooms and stir them rapidly over medium-high heat until they are all coated with the oil and lightly browned. Add to the bread mixture and stir in the seasonings. Mix everything with your hands until well combined.

This makes enough to stuff a huge bird with some left for baking in a dish.

SOURDOUGH SESAME CRACKERS

½   cup sourdough starter
2   tablespoons butter
2   teaspoons salt
1   cup unbleached white flour
¼   cup sesame seeds (preferably unhulled)

Allow the starter to stand at room temperature for several hours until it is frothy and active. Melt and cool the shortening and add it to the starter, along with the salt and as much of the flour as you can work in. When you have a very stiff dough, turn it onto a floured board and knead in the sesame seeds and, if needed, flour. This will be easier to do if a few minutes before kneading you allow the dough to rest, covered with a damp cloth.

When you have a very stiff dough, roll it to a uniform thickness of about ¹⁄₁₆ inch. Don't worry if the dough doesn't hold all the sesame seeds. Cut the crackers with a sharp, round cutter and arrange them on an ungreased cookie sheet, leaving space between each cracker. Stick them full of holes with a fork and bake in a preheated 400°F oven for about 7 minutes. The crackers should brown lightly, but don't let them over brown.

Cool the crackers on wire racks. If you can get them put away before everyone gobbles them, store them in an airtight tin.

SOURDOUGH CHERRY COBBLER

You may be surprised to see that this recipe calls for canned cherry pie filling. If you have cherries, you can make your own filling by adding sugar and thickening according to any standard cherry pie filling recipe. However, cherry pie filling seems to be one of the few prepared foods which are nearly as good from the store as you can make yourself, so if you're in a hurry, don't feel guilty about using the canned filling.

1	can cherry pie filling (1 lb. 5 oz.)
½	cup white raisins
¼	cup sourdough starter
¾	cup white flour
½	cup brown sugar
½	cup granulated sugar
¼	cup butter
½	cup chopped pecans

Grease an 8-inch round pie plate or cake pan. Put in the cherry filling and scatter raisins evenly over top of the cherries. Bring the sourdough starter to room temperature. When it is active and bubbling you can begin to mix the cobbler topping. Sift together the dry ingredients and cut in the butter until the mixture resembles coarse meal. Stir in the starter and the pecans. Mix thoroughly but lightly. Spoon the starter mixture over the top of the cherry filling, working in circles from the outer edges of the pan so that you end up with a small uncovered circle in the center.

Bake in a preheated 425°F oven for 25 minutes, or until the top is lightly browned and the cherry filling is bubbling up through the center. Serve barely warm with vanilla ice cream on top.

Makes 6 to 8 servings depending on how hungry everyone is for dessert.

SOURDOUGH PEANUT-OAT JUMBLE COOKIES

½   cup butter
½   cup vegetable shortening
1   cup granulated sugar
½   cup brown sugar
1   egg
¼   cup water
1   cup sourdough starter
1   teaspoon vanilla
½   teaspoon baking soda
1   teaspoon salt
1   cup white flour
2½ cups raw rolled oats
1   cup raw peanuts

Bring the starter to room temperature in a large bowl and allow it to become active before beginning to mix cookies. In a second bowl cream together the shortenings and sugars until fluffy, then beat in the egg and water. Beat well. With a wooden spoon mix in the sourdough starter, vanilla, soda, salt and flour. Stir until everything is well combined. Work in the rolled oats gradually. The batter will be quite thick by this time.

Lightly brown the peanuts in the oven or by shaking them in a hot skillet. Do not add fat or salt to them. When they have cooled, stir them into the dough.

Drop the dough by teaspoonsful onto a well greased cookie sheet. Leave space for the cookies to flatten and spread as they bake. Bake in a preheated 400°F oven for about 10 minutes, or until the cookies are brown. Cool the cookies on a rack before serving or storing.

MAKES ABOUT 36 COOKIES.

STRAWBERRY SHORTCAKE

This is a recipe for a true old-fashioned shortcake made with biscuits rather than white cake which has taken its place in recent years. When you have fresh strawberries and real cream for whipping to serve on these shortcakes, it's hard to imagine a finer dessert.

1	cup sourdough starter
1½	cups unbleached white flour
1	cup water
1¾	cups unbleached white flour
¼	cup sugar
2	teaspoons baking powder
½	teaspoon salt
½	cup butter

Mix together the first 3 ingredients in a large bowl and set aside, loosely covered, to ferment for up to 24 hours. When ready to bake the shortcakes, sift together the dry ingredients in another bowl, cut in the butter until the mixture is the consistency of coarse meal and then stir in the starter mixture.

When the dough is mixed as well as you can manage with a spoon, turn it out onto a floured board and *immediately* knead it. Work the dough quickly and lightly and only as much as necessary to make it hold together, then shape it into a ball and flatten it out with your hands to a little less than an inch thick. Use a large biscuit cutter or a soup can with both ends cut off to cut out the shortcakes. Put them on a greased cookie sheet, leaving space between each one. Brush the shortcakes with melted butter and cover with a lightweight damp cloth. Allow to rise in a warm place for 2 hours, then bake in a pre-heated 425°F oven for about 15 minutes. Serve the shortcakes slightly warm, topped with cold strawberries which have been mixed with a little sugar and lots of real whipped cream.

SOURDOUGH CHOCOLATE CAKE

Few people bother to bake cakes from scratch anymore unless they can produce something that's not possible with a mix. This sourdough chocolate cake falls in that category. It's got a fudge-like quality you can't get any way except with sourdough and since it's all mixed in one bowl, it's almost as easy as a boxed cake.

½	cup sourdough starter
1½	cups all purpose white flour
2	cups sugar
¾	cup powdered cocoa (not instant)
1	teaspoon baking powder
2	teaspoons baking soda
2	eggs
1	cup milk
½	cup vegetable oil
¾	cup cold coffee
1	teaspoon vanilla

Put the starter in a large bowl, cover loosely and allow to stand at room temperature until active and bubbling — at least an hour. Then add the rest of the ingredients, in the order given, beating well after each addition. It is not necessary to sift or premix any of the ingredients as long as you are careful to get the baking powder and baking soda evenly mixed.

Grease and flour two 9-inch round cake pans, pour in the batter, which will be thin, and bake in a preheated 350°F oven for about 30 minutes, or until the layers test done when poked with a toothpick. The cake will have pulled away from the sides of the pan.

Allow to cool about 10 minutes before removing from pans, then finish cooling the layers on wire racks. Do not frost until the cake is completely cold.

A mild chocolate butter cream frosting is nice with this cake.